False Claims of Colonial Thieves

False Claims of Colonial Thieves

Charmaine Papertalk Green

and

John Kinsella

First published 2018, reprinted 2018, 2020, 2021, 2022 x2
Magabala Books Aboriginal Corporation, Broome, Western Australia
Website: www.magabala.com
Email: sales@magabala.com

Magabala Books is supported by the Commonwealth Government through the Australia Council, and the State of Western Australia through the Department of Local Government, Sport and Cultural Industries. Magabala Books would like to acknowledge the generous support of the Shire of Broome, Western Australia.

Cover Design Design by Committee
Typeset in 11.5/14 pt Adobe Garamond Regular by Post Pre-press Group, Brisbane
Printed in Australia by Griffin Press Pty Ltd

Cataloguing-in-Publication data available from the National Library of Australia

Cover Image: *We Remember – Our Barna!* By Charmaine Papertalk Green and Mark Smith. This print tells the story of Geraldton's foundation around colonialism and its impact on the First Peoples – the Wilunyu of the Yamaji Nation. Colonial structures built on traditional campsites, forced the traditional occupiers out of their long held space to become onlookers of where they once lived – sang, slept, ate, danced and yarned. Colonial and contemporary structures only hide the surface but not the memory or connection of Yamaji to their land, 2016.

Dedicated to my brothers, Charles E Harvey (dec),
Alex Green, twins – Peter and John Green (dec),
Carl Green and Junior Green
CPG

Dedicated to Kim Scott
JK

Contents

Prologue

The stakeholders want their environmental scientists to deliver
flora and fauna on a platter, and they will do so for a price.
Stygofauna speak up through the land; some listen, more don't.

And so the mining companies reach into our schools,
funding programs that make students in their own image,
filling the holes they make in country with propaganda
sold as learning, gatekeeping into the church of university.

JK

*

Prologue Response

Privilege blindness
if environmental scientists say so
water comes from a plastic bottle
what lies on or within country
cannot be seen for the
privileged are privilege blind

CPG

Undermining

I

The king brown does not die from its own poison – within its body, inert.

Uranium within the hold of old ground around Wiluna is more than history. Leave it there. Intact.

The roo-tails sign the ground with making, and then they move on and back until stopped in their tracks.

We try to find our way through the world avoiding reactors. Terms of trade are weapons-grade.

Or see the range folding inwards, burst back out. Scrub, forests, their contents. All gone. Hole.

Lure of the material – to conjure empathy out of furnaces. Giving rise to religions honed as bayonets.

Quarry expanding to echo round owl rock its footing shaky and mice sharp as shrapnel.

JK

*

2.

Balu winja barna real winja
Real old ones them ones
Old ground our country
With ancient ones deep within
Wrapped tightly away
For the earth protecting
Itself from itself knowing
It can die from its own poison
Earth's silver grey hair
Elder belonging to a time
When the earth was soft
The little boy went to sleep
Balu winja barna real winja
Real old ones them ones
Man is a greedy monster
Interfering to satisfy self
Pulling old ones to surface
Birthing a dangerous little boy
Naming after a god and
Worshipping like a god
For the warfare toys of
Other little boys worldwide
Energy, power, death, destruction and money
Uranium is safe in the earth
Like a sleeping Elder
Balu winja barna real winja
Real old ones them ones

CPG

Grandmothers

My grandmother was a mining town child –
Kookynie where her father was foreman
of the South Champion Mine. My father
worked for decades in Karratha and Kal –
so it's not as if I come to the mines
without foreknowledge. But I can only
see them as the harrowing of Hell,
the opening of the land to release
what shouldn't be released,
a desecration of spirit and place.
This is no small-scale intrusion
for the sake of community,
but open slather, a ripping out,
an extraction to fuel the world's end.

JK

*

My grandmother washed
White town fella's clothes
To feed her kids and survive
I don't think mining would have
Meant much to her when
Trying to survive on the fringes
Of the Mullewa township
She had passed on by
The time Western Mining
Started destroying country

Out pass Morawa way
I saw the rail wagons as a kid
Rolling on by Maley Street
Carrying Koolanooka iron ore
Not understanding what this meant
Or where this country was going
Or why they wanted this country
I was just a kid watching trains

CPG

*

My grandmother's home is gone now
though plaques with her words,
her memories, stand among the tailings.
She would tell me the story of her
father lost in the desert being saved
by an Elder and Afghan cameleer.

As a child, I was obsessed with this
story and it made the dry spaces
lush and hopeful. In my great-
grandfather's delirium, he heard
the many voices of the desert,
knew the dry surface was only
one truth, that deep below
when they dug, the waters
of the desert flooded the shafts.

Nothing was as it seemed to him,
his workers. He knew the language

he couldn't understand was so complex
it was drawn out of the rock, the plants,
the very essence of the ground he was
robbing. And then the miner's disease
got his lungs, and he died in the hills
outside Perth, a long way from his
understanding, a long way from where
I think he started to know.

Those of us with colonisers
as ancestors look for ways to retell
their stories, to build hope. But the fact
is in the railway, the ore crushers,
the shafts sunk into country.

My grandmother told me many stories
of the desert. Of flowers and birds
on the edges. I am free to retell her stories.
She made no claim: she let them grow.
    I own none of them.
She told me she 'watched the blackfellas'
through the hessian curtains, watched
them go out past the town limits,
out past the claims, out beyond
the furthest wanderings of the prospectors,
out where there was a truth she knew
was so close to home, if only
    she understood how to see.

JK

*

There were no nanna Alice stories
Mum didn't talk lots about nanna
I think it hurt too much for my mum
To even utter her mother's name
It was not allowed in those days
When someone died their name died
At least the Native Welfare files
Kind of brought nanna Alice to life
Nanna was 42 when she died
I sit at her grave in Geraldton
Whispering secrets to a nanna
Telling her stories of country
Her descendants and their lives
I am glad the only mining
She would have known was
From the rich ochre on her
Body and in her hair during
Ceremony time out on country

CPG

Don't want me to talk

You don't want me to talk about
Mining or its impact on Country
You don't want me to talk about
The concept and construct of 'whiteness'
Its dominance and power in society
You don't want me to talk about
The art vultures here and everywhere
Modern day missionaries
Saving us on the great white canvas
You don't want me to talk about
Invasion of this land or a Treaty
It's a shared true history – let's heal
You don't want me to talk about
Past injustices, cultural cruelty, cultural genocide
And the cultural pain that is left behind
It's a shared true history – let us heal
You don't want me to talk about
How reconciliation could be the wrong word
On its own and without truth
You don't want me to talk about
Native titles process being for the white man
You don't want me to talk at all
Most of the time – you have your 'exotic' pets
You want me to nod, smile and listen to you
And it doesn't really matter if I don't hear you
You don't want me to talk about
How I have got a voice
And you don't listen

CPG

Dream mine time animals

Contemporary mechanical dream mine time animals
Creating sacred sites for the future
Is what our kids will proudly tell
Their stories around the campfires
Of the mechanical snakes slithering across land
Creating new traditional pathways and song lines
Transporting hills and country to the coast
Filling the belly of monstrous steel fish
Vomiting our precious earth onto foreign shores

Contemporary mechanical mine dream time animals
Hills broken into millions of pieces
Deep cuts into the flesh of earth
Gaping wounds with polluted waterholes
Haulpak mechanical dream mine time animals
Moving defenceless country from country
The remnants of sacred sites given up for money
Man-made hills our children will claim as belonging
To country, tradition and culture
False hills they will weave into song lines
And cultural boundary markers
Dream mine time animal's destroyer of land

CPG

Country rulers

In this country of milk and money
And iron ore, iron ore
Mining, mining and more mining
Who are the real rulers of country?
What does our voting really give us?
We are sucked into some false sense of decision making
But this club of country rulers
Holding court are mainly white
Several could have touch of the tar brush
Australia is hung up on skin colour
Closet skeletons are carefully guarded
Especially the black kind
Lands stolen from traditional owners
Land protected for thousands not hundreds
Thousands and thousands of years
I forgot land was not owned before
Society only existed at time of invasion
Whatever existed before did not count
They all have an Aboriginal story
Entwined in their family history
Of course – of bloody course
Who do you think showed their
Grandparents or parents this rich land
Bullshit they stumbled across it one day
They lived in harsh environments
With the true land owners
Then they stole it

CPG

Selfish warriors

On one hand they want to fight
To protect country and rights
But with other hand they shake the
Hand of resource cheque books
What are they doing – for goodness sake?
How much land they gonna let them take?

In one breath fighting for land
In the other just letting it all go
Like a little kid playing games
Sulking in the sand pit – whimpering
"Give me what I want and then you can …"

Dig it up
Blow it up
Crush it up
Poison it up
Ship it out
Do what you want

Gimme money money money
Car four wheel drive car

Selfish warrior don't really care
If once did that's gone into the air
Polish the boots and iron the pants
Ore iron ore iron the white man wants more

Groom the beard get ready to shine
Selfish warrior now belongs to the mines

CPG

Fe Fi Fo Fum

Fe fi fo fum
I smell a mining robot chum
Marching to the beat
Of the resource drum
Airport stampede of
Yellow, silver, orange, gold
Time with family, community,
Children now sold sold sold
Into planes to move about
To many mine sites no doubt
Barna being destroyed in WA State
Rolling in dough to fill their plate
Grinding the land to make this bread
Land protection and Aboriginal rights
The last thing in their heads
Greedy dirty mining dynasty's
Everything but money is very dead

Fe fi fo fum
Decked out in flouros
Here they come
I smell a mining robot chum

CPG

Fluoro girl world

I am not a fluoro girl
Living in a fluoro world
Driving a big truck
Making big mining bucks
Loving the navy orange look
Working for the mining crooks

I'm not a fluoro girl
I don't live in a fluoro world
That life is not fantastic

CPG

Don't mine me

Don't mind me Australia
I just don't care for mining
And your colonial bulldust
I think all the time about minding
This land for the next generations
Am I allowed to do that?

Your stole our barna, country, land
And still stealing under the name of

King
Queen
Government
Economy
Asia
PROFIT

Don't mind me Australia
While you are busy
Sticking explosives everywhere
Getting a hard on from blowing up land
Pumping chemicals deep into mother
Drip feeding our waters with poison
Waving goodbye to animals and plants
Contaminating all that you touch

Don't mind me and don't mine me

CPG

Niagara Dam Poems: Eastern Goldfields Western Australia (Wongai Country)

1 Floodways in desert

In the floodways
where my grandmother
played as a child:
rare water on the edge
of the desert hinted
at in dry riverbeds,
a great drier lighter hinterland;
whitewashed red
and orange sandstone,
wagtails over the Rubicon,
'the die is cast',
gold and mines so deep
they drowned.

2 Revamped

Against the grey skin
of the dam wall,
raised up
from the brittle dry
for steam-trains
green water
corrodes: under
ledges, the underbanks,
fairy-martins hangnest

where humidity
encourages midgies
to swarm, roo scats
on the miniature cliffs,
fires where circling
has revamped
pioneer myths.

3 On the desert shores

Moonscape sandstone
on the shores of Niagara –
rose quartz
apricot quartz
scattered finds
(sheoaks warp as a rare front darkens over)
smoothed but crumbling edges
on edges, mandala succulent plants eating
stone; the less we name
desert plants troubled
at gatherings of water,
the more erosion
backfills space,
young grebe
on what is now
rippled blue-black surface,
glancing at array
of rock as another's geology.

4 Night parrots affront

The front that almost reaches
this interior, wind driving hard
from southwest to vibrate
feathers of zebra finches
in sensory overload,
anticipation of rain event
as heavens can-opener camper vans
of the *Around Australia* crews,
pipping them at posts.

Rain falls lightly
and holding off
                              absence
is the night parrot
affronting accomplices

here in force
                        in the middle
of a rare dark day
though lightning against the glare.

JK

The Salt Chronicles

I Aloneness

I realise: so often
I write myself alone
as if no one would go there
for its own sake: they might
for science, or surveillance,
reflecting on their loss,
the irony of making more land
less arable, or maybe
tree-planting.

I went there
to enclose in an open-ended
environment, where earth-cracks
from the tearing were gateways
to a journey: social
misunderstanding at school,
competitive sport,
rivalry; centre of the earth.

The formation of a salt crystal
is bridge and timeline to tether
astronomy and forecasting,
to mirror then encrust then paper the bones
of rodents, small marsupials, birds:
the familial breakdown.
Of myself, I was sure:
the tufts of survivor grass,

the resilient spiked trees
stunted and wind-bent,
samphire on the edges and elevations,
marsh grasses slung with Christmas spiders,
stalked by plovers and herons.
In the brine the tumbles of larvae,
crustaceans that shouldn't have survived the salt,
species created in a few seasons
then lost.

2 Salt Wraiths

Salt wraiths leave trails –
salt breaking through clean ground.
Where the salt saturates
they are the white ache
of pillars, arches, sheets:
embedded as insect corpse
or blown seed of wild oats.
At night, they make
a chemical heat.

Of no order,
they connect with nothing but salt
leaching up, or running
underground passages:
above, the owl strikes quick
in its fearlessness,
but flies below the moon
hoping to swoop
out of the wraiths' sonar-

blip, a clash of technologies,
the wraiths emanating
from the ground up,
they take hold
bit by bit,
the owl complies
digesting the mouse,
the night's castings.

X-raying for animal and mineral presence
written stages of sedimentary formation
wraiths imagine they know
others – have known song and conversation,
charred criteria of fires; oil lines
blurred in salt buffers, a slush
of samphire crusting
as dryness set dimensions
in rip-up-marks to break it up,
iterations of sheoak
whispers, such small seedlings
to get a hold, but if they do they flourish
and serve to strain; in dispossessing
wraiths might think they displace
but dialogues about the feeding of the river
by salt creeks that will drive out the serpent
are persistent; it's the wraith's indifference
I missed as a child wandering
the first-degree sunburn
and thinking hallucinations
were prophets or ghosts; in the blaze of white
I lost definitions; a long way north
it's as if focus was made through Bradshaw

bothering to record when 17,000 years
was a dynamic counterpoint
in itself.

The air is fetid about the gullies' throat:
the rubbish used to throttle
erosion: they batter negatives
against the resistant plates,
these emanations of electrolysis,
afterimages we pick up on
when alone and receptive,
further out in the blanks
it sterilises.

3 Mapping and Companionship

Sketched on graph paper
intended for school, red lines
mark salt seams, blue lines
hard clear water
of gullies and creeks,
green the algal displays
inside their aquariums.
In the drawing out
so some might follow
as nemesis said or echo
in the mirror, or Diana
perved on from afar by binoculars,
or the memory of salt crackle underfoot
the tinnitus that scratches and flutters
like half-formed auditory

hallucinations; fight as much as we did,
my brother and I would go out there in maps
of our ulterior making, and 'own' what cousins
'owned' by right of family, and 'own'
the fragile nature of the eroding
footholds, lines of wash
from paddocks still yielding
good crops though closer
to granite cap-rock
year in, year out,
marked on bedheads
by brass shell casings,
sharp lights like the green-gold glow
of navigation markers
dropped by passing aircraft.

4 Contrary

I cannot look at salt
on the crumbling winter roads
of Ohio without it causing
dislocation, a deep disturbance
in what might happen,
a shifting of sensibilities,
a fraught transaction –
even pain.

The salt that hardens arteries,
the salt whose lack has the shearer crippled
on the shed floor, kicking like a wether.

The agistment of salt mines
and the way sweat and blood
dissolve with history: the paranoia
that says underneath it all
must be holes in the text,
Macherey's unconscious urge to
see the oppression of salt licks,
sheep huddled around the drum,
cobalt in their bellies,
manipulating salt taxes,
the market value,
salerium argentium,
the enforced purchase of salt
by children eight years or over,
straddling ant trails
reaching into dead zones
where insects drop
from airspace
and are collected,
collated.

5 Salt Pans at Dampier: Company Semi-Fact Sheet

It takes 18 months
to put the salt
through
its evaporative cycle.
Algae are 'contained'
by milkfish
bred to scour the ponds,
to run the mirrors

of sunshine that turn
sight inside out.
Dampier Salt = Rio Tinto 65%
Marubeni 20%
Nissho-Iwai Ltd 10%
Itochu Corporation 4.5%.
They enjoy the nearby
gas deposits, the export of iron ore
through the heaviest tonnage-
capable port in Australia.
The salt ponds = 100 square kilometres.
Magnesium sulphate,
magnesium chloride,
potassium chloride.
World price for bromides
not adequate.
My father managed the workshop
keeping the belly dumping trailers
for the giant salt trucks –
and the Kenworth
prime movers themselves
in good working order.
Management, he wasn't Union,
but respected Union labour
well enough, but 'not the blokes who'd
go out at the drop of a hat …'
he tells me this twenty-six
years later – knowing I'd be Union
as the salt drives his blood pressure,
hijacks his sarcasm.

JK

Red Lead, Almost Dead

Lead tetroxide bold as … lead
in the lab, my lab, my phase transition
of poisoned exploration, discovery.
Bought from Selby's in the big jar,
enough to make a crystal palace, kookaburra
feature window portal out of the gabled
house, but mainly for completion (a *collectable*),
the danger, addition to the hellzone
of thorium nitrate and mercury (mobs
of sheep don't 'split like mercury'; they are
broken and forced apart, made to rejoin,
to meld again). Or crucibles of pure lead,
lustrous liquid for sinkers, bullets
(reloading one's own), the vapour haze, dumbing
down as bright spark focuses the Bunsen's
flame and draws all in, organic and inorganic
testcase, what's left is the shame, splitshot
chomped onto line, wire-snipped flex
off the great rolled sheet, a wad of dull
grey chewing gum. Lead light, lead
unwrapped from yellowcake, the play
of radiation and decay, the age-old
age of earth, signifier of longevity
you won't enjoy, complete, as body
at least. But red lead, magnificently
useless in the shed lab (ah! the Mettler
balance!), glows and sits heavy
on the shelf, begging to be mixed
with anything that will change its outlook.

Fuming acids. Hydrochloric dissolute
in the gut as well. Try everything. Make dissolve.
This the legacy, the effect. Resolve,
colour code. Dull red throb. Dead red lead.

JK

Histories

My mother taught us respect.
The conversation has never ended.

1

When the stookers
Came in from the Reserve
I was tasked with taking
The water out during smoko –
Kids my own age reached out
To take the sky from my hands,
Or to give it to me, which they did.

2

My memories
Aren't like anyone else's, mostly.
Though they overlap with my brother's
A lot – he was also unseeing
The world we were taught at school,
And he was listening askew,
Looking closer, knowing
Where not to go.

3

The imagists cut things back
To bare essentials – but here,
I take the essence of the bush
And make false claims
If I turn a bird into an image,
Co-opt its names.

4

Working the wheatbins
At Mingenew I heard
A white South African
Truck driver and a bunch
Of the local white boys
Were going to shoot up
A 'tin shack' on the edge
Of town late at night.
I tried to stop them –
They ran me out of town.
I hid in the bush till daylight.
They drove around searching.
Managed to hitch a lift to Perth.
Heard they went on their
Hunting spree unopposed.

5

I swap letters
With a relative
Doing time – he tells
Me he reads my words
To his cellmate who is Noongar.
He says my letters bring them comfort.
He from the distance of inside,
Me from the distance of outside.
All of us trying to say something
About imprisonment, its legacy.

6

My father's house 'Up North'.
His politics of the mines,
Of management in the trucking
Division. Those mechanics
Working under him, the politics
Of labour. As teenagers
We travelled to Millstream
With him and saw light in rock:
Not reflections, but the secret
Sought by the rapacious,
Sought out so hard but never found –
They disappear mountains
And turn them into cars.

7

There was a carved emu egg,
A boab nut etched with fire,
And, believe it or not,
'An Albert Namatjira'
Hanging in the lounge room
Alongside the footy pennants.
You couldn't say those folk
Were anything but white fellas,
But under the murk of their talk
Something was happening –
Something in need
Of conversion.

8

The new kid from southern USA
Who said, 'I've plenty of experience
Fighting blacks where I come from.
I know what to expect, let me at them.'
Weirdly, he had a kind of sick respect
In his racism, believing in the quality
Of the opposition, seeing the world
As two-toned shoes designed
For stomping.

9

Language and the bush –
We heard the words and knew
Poetry as an artform
Was intended to make up
For what was lost in the taking.

Language and the bush –
The words weren't just lists,
They went into the essence
As we searched nature guides
For explanations they didn't have.

10

The Golden Gloves boxer
Watched over us when we
Arrived in Carnarvon
From Geraldton. The
White fellas here
Drink and prey
On their own.
He said. He said.

11

Thanks you mob
For giving me a roof
To sleep under

When no one else
But my mother
And brother
Would give me
The time of day.
I said I'd never
Forget it. I said,
Uncle, I did, I said,
No bullshit, I promise.

12

Vigilantes
Gather
At the edge
Of the Super Pit – dug
Out to undermine
Their own footing.

Burrowing deep,
Extracting gold
To make it no more
Than bullion – the veins
Of the earth
Uprooted.

And the killer
Goes off-site,
Chases a kid
To his death.
And the earth
Cries out of the dry,

And the vigilantes
Block their ears.
And the elegies
Fill the streets.
And the Pit eats itself
Twenty-four hours a day.

JK

Hawes – God's Intruder

1

The church Hawes made in Mullewa
was great in its stone and earth.
The white folk praised its God-
shape out in the hot zone.
He got a lot of credit.
A lot of praise.
His altar had believers
kneeling on ants.
Red-tailed black cockatoos
sat on its edges. Visitors
didn't know their names.

JK

2

Galloping in, bible and cross in hand
Hawes, God's intruder
Altar stone of the earth
Intruding on our barna
In the name of Catholicism
Bow your head and conform
For this is now the whiteworld
Hawes, God's intruder
Onto our barna
A campsite – home

A place of living
A place of our ceremonies
Long before it was
called Mass Rock
Hawes, God's intruder

CPG

3

Coming in from the 30,000 acres,
eyes fixed on the ornate structure,
as if two towns – or more – divided
like the biblical sea, shearing teams
drinking the red fleeces away.

Not our church, someone said,
and we wondered, as Dad
got his supplies of beer
from the Railway Hotel,
his hands oily from the dual-wheeled tractors,
burnt from working in the superphosphate shed,
the fog of occupation over the fortunes of country,
not his, not the millionaire's
whose farm he managed.

That priest, England in his veins,
converted the midwest diocesan vision
of souls gathered under one-roofs.
A Spanish breeze drawn
under the arches. Mt Carmel.

Where? Romanesque?
What did he write: 'My heart
is in these stones'? His European
heart? His heart of … home?

And we as kids, outsiders,
jumping from one side of the tracks
to the other. *The Mullewa*,
train to Perth, discontinued
a few years earlier.

JK

4

Living on the Mullewa fringes
Became my people's place
When a colonial township emerged
Like a pimple in the wildflowers

Foreign church structures rose
Dominating the landscape
Family showed me the quarry
From which rocks were taken
Building the Whiteman's worship place
Mullewa Reserve nearby
Along the Mullewa – Morawa Road
Aboriginal hands helped build that temple
Their energy and sweat is in them rocks
Their heart is in them rocks
Hawes didn't do it on his own

Wonder if that is written anywhere?
As a child I peered into that
Curious why gargoyles watched the entry
Frightened to look at the statues inside

Our playgrounds included train tracks,
Wheat silos, the Common and looking into the dam
As local kids we would
Peer through the dam's big wire fence
Thinking of our family who died in there
We were told not to forget them
The sadness in family voices
Inside the dam was a no go zone

Wildflower season meant tourist buses
We chased from Our Lady of Mt Carmel
To the Lesser Hall for the promise
Of leftover sandwiches and cakes.

CPG

5

On the steps of the Big Church
I hesitate, unsure of what's inside
for me. I have the sand and wheat
ships in my head, and wonder
how far they might stretch the scene.

Mum is a teacher at the high school,
and my nickname there is Dictionary.

I write poems in a laboratory.
I work weekends and holidays
in the shadows of the mineral sands
factories, preparing samples
that show the quality of the land
pouring through the capitalist
hourglass, shifting the spirit
to metals and plastics and paint.

It was rocket science. The birds
stayed away and their songs
ignored by too many. Shifting
sands. Gunslits in settler buildings.

We ride our bikes from town
to Drummond's Cove where crayfish
bristle below and reef sharks
patrol the gaps, snapper glinting,
brightening the underworld.

We live opposite the prison
in a limestone house – colonial mansion –
once home to nurses,
taken over by the Education
Department, a statement of possession
we know is haunted, distressed.
We weather a cyclone,
we find old coins fallen
through the wooden boards.

We are part of something
we can't quite piece together.
Mum volunteers to teach prisoners
written English, to listen to their lives.

Now, where house and yard
and Moreton Bay fig stood,
is Coles Shopping Centre
carpark.

Down from there, trains
rounded on themselves,
head-to-tail on the turntable,
and the sea against the seawall,
and the curve of beach
reaching to St George's
(what did he have to do with it?)
and the cobbler's sting that undid
my nerves and had me shrieking
the agony of Champion Bay
I didn't understand. The school
was busy re-enacting Grey's
expedition but I knew
that wasn't part of my vision,
though later I'd rewrite it
as a poem of decolonisation.

When I return to Geraldton,
to what part of me is there,
I rest in a dry creek bed
and listen to the river redgums,

I go to the bottomless pool
and watch the swallows
defy gravity. I know sunsets
make a coast and I listen
hoping my errors
will find redress.

JK

6

Growing up I lived opposite the Catholic Church
Our Lady of Mt Carmel in Mullewa
Every day I walked past Monsignor's house
I knew nothing of their beliefs and customs
It was just a playground to take pictures
Get a cool drink from the water fountain
The gargoyles perched at the entrance
Frightened me at night as I closed my eyes
And sprinted past the church to get home
I didn't understand why these monsters
Were on a church building roof –
Looking out of place

During the celebrated wildflower season
We would cute little Aboriginal kids pose
For the tourists as we waited for rewards
Of cakes and sandwiches leftovers from
Their morning and afternoon teas
They probably felt sad for us – who knows!
We just got our feed and waved to them

I wrote poems and stories in a little diary
You know the ones with lock and key
And cute teenage girly covers
Each time finding new hiding places
From intruding little relatives and the rest
Each time having to tear up and throw away
My words, thoughts, emotions, feelings
Because there were no hiding places

The big church in Geraldton on the sand hill
Was not part of my world in Mullewa
Our SDA church sat staunchly
On Maitland Road waiting for its family
We got bags of Weet-bix, oranges, and apples
Saved us from really starving so
That's something I guess

But that big church in Geraldton
What a poser standing there like a temple
My mum went to a wedding there in the 1940s
An Aboriginal Catholic wedding at that
I have a pic of mum leaning on church outside wall
All young beautiful and a tea maid
Mum had a permit to work in Geraldton
At West End of Marine Terrace
From the Native Protection Board
Or should I say her Employer had the permit
That's the way it was – Aboriginal people
Were controlled and couldn't move freely

As a teenager going across to the
Aboriginal Basketball carnivals
Or at the Maitland Park footy oval
I don't recall the Big Church

Later I moved to Geraldton
And the Big Church was in my face
I drove past it, I walked past it
I stared at it from the
Queens Park Theatre lawns

And what learned about it made me sick
The space it so grandly took over
Was once a traditional campsite
The Aboriginal people were
Moved to other locations like
Moore River Native Mission
Social engineering of our people
And colonisers land grab take over
Is said to have happened at same time

Oh yes the Big Church is grand
They pray and worship their god
Tourists come from everywhere
With their cameras to make memories

All I can think about when I see it
Is of the campsite taken over
Of our people displaced and alienated
From traditional country
Colonised space it became and stayed

CPG

7

The night I was beaten so badly
the cops and ambulance arrived
at the Geraldton Drives to carry
me away from my comfort zone,
I gained a weird respect from
a Yamaji guy who stood watching
while a white boy who hated
my guts pounded my head
into the bitumen, chips of blue
metal lodging in my scalp
like a sick halo lit-up by
the flickering images
of The Who's 'Pinball Wizard' –
Tommy playing on the big
screen like out of control
dreams and imaginings.
The Yamaji guy said
to his white associate,
You better stop, mate,
(there was only the mateship
of being out at night and searching
for action in the dead rural suburbs,
the beaches just too far away
to catch the echoes of waves)
he said, There's too much blood,
you can't even see his face
it's so messed up. It's mush.
I heard him speak as cars
of whites sat watching,
without losing a beat,

the 'crazy flipper fingers',
and the guy doing the punching –
a schoolmate – got a few extra
in and then gave it away,
my brother screaming,
restrained by others
in the group – the gang.
That beating changed my face
and my life. I'd climbed over the fence
with my brother and a friend,
and spread a blanket up front
with a speaker next to us,
swigging green ginger wine.
We'd offered the boys
who'd come in the same way
from a different angle,
a drink. Then the Dictionary-
teacher's-son-stuff came out
and it turned bad. When the cops
wanted names they weren't interested
in the white kid who'd done
the damage, but wanted to know
if there'd been any 'black bastards'
in the gang. I said no, just whites,
and didn't name names. For some reason
I wondered if they were pines
planted alongside the drive,
inland, to hide the screen.
What sort of trees are they?
I asked, and the cops thought
I had brain damage. I still
can't remember, though

my brother lived for years
near where the old screen had stood,
and I looked in, trying
to reconfigure. Years later,
the Yamaji guy saw me and said,
You're a legend, bro – we –
we – know you didn't tell the cops
anything. I know you kept me out of it.
If you hadn't, my whole family
would have paid and would still
be paying. In your name crimes
beyond imagining would
have been committed.

JK

8

Aah I remember the sickly taste
Of green ginger wine
Sitting in the tall grass sipping
Or on the hill behind the Club Hotel
Yarning about young girl things
Giggling, getting light headed
Now I ask myself
How did 13-year-old girls get grog?
Where did we even get the money?
Can't remember; all I know it happened
And I seen some pretty good smashes
Across on medicine square
You know real fights

Back then when fair fights happened
Fights were picked up at sun up
To satisfy someone's need to be satisfied
Not this mobbing bar rushing shit
With gings, bottles and stones
Or the kicking in the head business
I seen men and women take it away
Clean and fair and with handshakes
White kids not in our sight
I think they had their own craziness
happening elsewhere in town
They really weren't my concern
My space was quite a blackout
If you know what I mean
A few of the Yamaji girls from the reserve
Looked out for me – never forgot that
That kind of respect lasts a lifetime
Even when they died far too young

CPG

9

We were in Northampton recently
and families were sheltering from the sun
under shop eaves – we crossed the road
to study the gothic of Hawes' St Mary's
in Ara Coeli and his Sacred Heart Convent
and then back across to where the old tennis
court brooded and now native vegetation
has been planted as if it was never there

in the first place. I think of the Tennis
Court Oath, the meeting of the Third
Estate locked out by Royalty, their pledge
to meet until a constitution was drawn-up
and I imagine a *Serment du Jeu de paume*
at Northampton as the town's stone buildings
summon the lead ore from the ground
to contaminate so much further than
the strongest eye can see, and I think of
the t-shirt you designed now hanging
in the Geraldton Maritime Museum
where the white woman selects the little one
in the middle but any one will do! her
own revolution in taste and vanity, in owner-
ship and protection and doing them a favour
rewriting of love and family, as architecture
is to poets and spiritual tourists, to miners
and collectors of Australiana. Then I am
back thirty-seven years doing the school
marathon trials up behind Geraldton Senior
High – up into dunes beyond
Shenton Road, down to the back beach
where time rips apart certainty, sandshoes
slipping in sand, and back past what
I now know is Hawes' Hermitage,
built in 1936 for his retirement
before he retreated to Cat Island
in the Bahamas … but we knew it
as the 'place where weirdos live', a haunted
hellish place we jogged past fast, where
bullies pushed you closer and a face
never defined peered at you from

the unnatural window in its gabled roof.
I read now its design was influenced
by the Arts and Crafts movement
of his home country, that it's what
architects call 'Inter-war Old English
style', and that it is a national treasure.
Our fear, the unspoken poisoning
of water by lead disturbed in the ground,
the stripped paddocks surrounding Northampton,
the surveying and renaming and theft
of bodies and souls are not treasures.
Families were sheltering from the sun
under shop eaves, and I swore
a non-violent oath where
the tennis courts
had played their role.

JK

10

Hawes' stone piles Mooniemia placed
Tidiness of a town – village with rolling hills
Standard creek for frogs to amuse
Hawes' Mooniemia stone construct
Forcing eyes to look upon its face and body
Like a sulking teenager demanding attention
out of place and knowing it
Fleeting glances from car windows
Is as close as I ever got
I imagine white ghosts of the pasts

Doing all the things White people do
Conforming to the rules of their society
I also wonder if Aunty (RIP) went in there
Hawes stone pile stamping Nhanda land for the settler
Where did the stones come from?
I think what our old people told us
'Dont take that rock or stone from there
Leave it don't take it away – no good'
Hawes with his religious amour
Quarried wherever he wanted so
That people will speak his name forever
To ensure fame is bestowed for the
Stone constructs strategically placed
The Yamaji architects with the clay and mud huts
Placed on the same land pre settler times
Are forgotten, not talked about, ghosts
Explorer Grey did document for us to find
To remind people of the first architects here
The Nhanda, Naaguja, Amangu, Nhanagardi
Whilst Hawes' stone piles cry out for attention
Throughout the Midwest and Yamaji areas
I feel sad about that – he will always have
His society's religion, a fan club of architects
Whilst our Yamaji culture and history is still
Not celebrated or appreciated for its place on the land
How can over 50,000 yrs mean nothing?
I wish our people's constructs could have been
National Treasures instead of on pages in
Surveyor accounts of land good to steal and claim
As a teenager in Mullewa I ran home past
Our Lady of Mt Carmel – this was my marathon
After school every day for many years

A fast sprint at night thinking of the gargoyles
With their wings and ugliness coming to get me
They played their role in keeping us out

CPG

Bottlebrush Behind Our Lady of Fatima Church, Nanson, Chapman Valley

Shriven with late afternoon rift-light? Sun levelling
the already levelled hills, honeyeaters and inland thornbills
raging around purple stone, and the Bishop calling Hawes

out as a difficult man, who once crossed could 'cut you dead'.
This resonates in deadly ways, and since working with Charmaine
on this array of monuments tapped into the region, such

concentrations of God, I can't help think that the birds are re-
consecrating the eroded rock and sand beneath our feet, stirred
by wings beating discriminately. Family photograph each other

under the bloody rills of bottlebrush flowers – capillaries
of an anatomy we track with borrowed knowledge, but with a shudder
as prayers shake down the land into farms and a cradle

of wheat, a crucible – and the ECHELON communications base
playing realpolitik lies – secrets of gross exploitation by clusters
of atomic warriors. And there's a droning in the air that resists

dispersal by sea-winds, from windmills spinning back
against their driving force. 'Surreal' – a trendy, easy word
that's seeped into the present and gets a working-over,

just like 'uncanny' – insists on being spoken, an intrusion that sends
the bungarra shooting off into the scrub as we prompt it to leave
the road. All of this, all of these conflations in the valley

where Hawes is still lauded, where the bottlebrushes roots
test the soil to see what's *really* changed, where the dead are cut out
of the imagery and a miracle is channelled to cement the gaps.

JK

Honey to Lips Bottlebrush

Young teachings perched on Walkaway hill
Space reclaiming decolonising respacing
Bottlebrush explosive red inviting eyes
Honey to lips or bush cordial sweet
    Honey to lips bottlebrush
    Kneeling at altar of God no
    Not on this land not here
Hawes-centricity another world away
Archived Greenough 12 kilometres west
Appetite not here for Hawes' mudpie
Young thirst for knowledge Yamaji
    Honey to lips bottlebrush
    Hawes turned wooden candlesticks
    Ghosts sit at Centro Greenough
    Not on this land not here
Sucking nectar bottlebrush sweet
Wattle seeds eating tasting time ago
Visions of firesticks ancestors' walking
Tracks etched into land across land
    Honey to lips bottlebrush
    Red fire dotted campsites
    Culture banished torment real
    Wheat grain money worshipped
    Not on this land not here
Dance ground feet sand reunite connect
Still wind still ancestors come to visit
Gentle kiss giving to young spirits

Reassuring for the onward journey
Right here on this land right here

CPG

Our Lady of Mt Carmel, Mullewa

'Mons. Hawes had a great affinity with the Aboriginal people of Mullewa but they were not comfortable in attending Mass in the local church.'
http://www.monsignorhawes.com.au/thebuildings_mullewaoutlady.html

We had to go back home that way, past the church
Hawes built stone by stone, as the colonial myth goes.
We had to go back home that way, because Mullewa
isn't the church, but the place where people live
across many conversations, and country isn't a cross
        or a survey marker.

We had to go back home that way, though I can't
visit the farm my father managed because it doesn't
seem right – wreath flowers on the roadside attracting
the wildflower visitors, though fencers have taken
out so much of the roadside vegetation the wreaths can't
        benefit from disturbance. Erasure.

We had to go back home that way, past the Marian
projection into the 'region', beaming out towards
the stony ground further and further – from the coast
inland inland following railway, road trains, the mucking
around in the school playground. All of that
        making the town, community.

We had to go back home that way to decode
our reasons, their irrelevance, the damaging. While
up on the caricature Romanesque tower – colonial theatre
of cruelty – a kestrel tracks martins fast off the eaves
while a bottlebrush sheds red we might, if we try, see as angry –
        not gargoyle warding-off, but kestrel drawing in.

We had to go back home that way, wondering
about the legacy of architecture, the caretaking
        of affinity.

JK

No other road

Home is back that way, there is no other
Mum's bush camp childhood home in sight
No need to drive there unless you belong
Mum shared water stories – having to cart it
Government well about two kilometres away
No house with tap running water for a
Cool drink on a hot Mullewa summer's day

Mass Rock is the intruder in our space
Mass Rock is not my significant site
My people's campsite not Hawes' space

Home is back that way, there is no other
Great grandmother buried along Mullewa north
Pioneer cemetery flattened by some idiot
Erasing evidence of topsoil markings
Final burial place of our Murgoo Elder

Mass Rock is the intruder in our space
Mass Rock is not my significant site
My people's campsite not Hawes' space

Home is back that way, there is no other
Man-made temple like peacock stands
Marker of a civilised yet uncivilised world
A space for those to pray their sins away
Under the watchful eyes of icons and statues
Like civilised colonial pagans with gargoyle guards

Mass Rock is the intruder in our space
Mass Rock is not my significant site
My people's campsite not Hawes' space

Home is back that way, there is no other

CPG

I don't like flying over

I don't like flying over Wadjemup
On the flight path to Geraldton
It doesn't comfort me looking down
Over the island others call Rottnest
I always scan the distance from mainland
Thinking of long ago in draconian times
Western Australian Aboriginal men sent here
Trapped 11 miles away from walking paths home
Forced to mine limestone to build a jail from hell
Chains around necks and roped together
Locals talk about Rotto, quokkas and Tentland
One can sleep on top of unmarked graves
This is not a holiday island
It's a prison memory of shootings
Hangings, drownings, measles, influenza
Such cruel colonial practices inflicted on our men
There cannot be a masterclass in amnesia
We must continue to remember
To honour the men who died out there
It is not a holiday place
No matter how much prettied up
Lots of spirits still there on Wadjemup

CPG

Wildflower Singing

Like a feast laid out
On a long table in
Front of me
My eyes welcome
The sight of my
Ancestral lands
Singing in wildflowers

CPG

Culture Bath

Immerse yourself in your culture
Let it wash over you
Bathe in it like you would
A bath filled with flowers
Let it flow into every
Cell of your being
Your culture will hold you
Your spirit will rejoice
Let you culture hold you
And never be a bystander
Don't look the other way
Don't be an observer
Embrace your culture with open arms
For it is your belonging

CPG

I won't pretend

I won't pretend it's easy
Living in an intercultural space
Cultural clashes and tensions
Bounce and collide
And sometimes explode
Trying to make sense
Of our ways of knowing
Of our ways of being
I won't pretend it's dull
Because it is not
It's so intense but culturally
Inspiring – rewarding
Reflecting on two cultures
How our lives are shaped
Not letting one culture take over
Finding time to walk over
Each other's barna

CPG

Campfire

A campfire binds us
Swapping yarns
Silly ones to make us laugh
Serious ones about our people
Sharing ones about our cultures
We share this space
Yamaji to Maori to Yamaji
Happy, content, relaxed together
We know it's not like this
In other parts of Australia
The youth fight each other
The newly arrived want to fit in
For a better life and nice life
So take on attitudes of white Australia
Do they know what they do
To the First Peoples of this barna?
Of course not everyone is like this
We carry on sharing our space
Knowing our space and our place
As Indigenous peoples
Sharing bacon bones and kangaroo meat

CPG

Tangi

The sadness we share
As I help prepare your mother
For the undertaker
It's not our way but it seems so natural
I have been with dead family before
But in the hospital ward
I know death very well
Just not at home – not this way
You tell me this is your people's way
The undertaker will bring her back
In a few hours to her family and home
Before her final journey from physical world
You tell me to join everyone
Come sit down on the mattress
Near the casket where she sleeps
Sing a song, tell a yarn
Shed a tear, sit and reflect
Or just be there
I wonder if her spirit is watching
This is not my way for three days
But it seems so natural, respectful
Comforting, cultural, right, protecting
But as night starts to creep in
My Yamaji mind starts to tell me other things
What spirits will come
Under this cover of darkness
Will they be good or bad?
Will they recognise me?
Will my spirit be weakened?

Who will protect me so far from
My barna and people?
In this land of the long white cloud
You tell me to join everyone
To sleep in this space
To be there with your mother
I tell you I am not disrespecting
I tell you this is not our way
Who will protect my spirit
In this far away land?
The sadness we share

CPG

Yamaji Culture

Yamaji culture
It's a culture worth loving
It's a culture worth fighting for
It's a culture worth being loved

Why tell me I don't need it?
Why tell me I can't need it?
Why tell me I can't love my culture?
Why tell me it's not worth fighting for?
Why tell me it's not worthy of love?

Yamaji culture
I love it – I laugh for it
I stress for it – I cry for it
I fight for it
I believe it is worthy
Of love and respect

Don't crawl into a
Dark corner of cultural nothingness
For your children
Grandchildren and descendants
Will blame you – blame you
For not caring enough
Or wanting your culture enough
Or loving and respecting it
Don't be that ancestor

I watch Yamaji culture change
It adapts to survive
Why don't you understand that?
Why can't you understand that?

Yamaji culture is a culture
Worth fighting for
A culture worth loving
A culture worthy
Don't wipe all that away
Hang on – hang on tight countrymen
To our Yamaji Culture

CPG

Lake Magic Resonances (January 2017)

for Tony Hughes-d'Aeth

1

Into the summer's flameless burn of night,
residues – and housed in the radar dish
of salt – such vast accumulations –
reception almost non-existent,
but hope rises into darkness
as night gives to creatures
outside the spotlight.

2

White branchings
up out of the bed of lack –
gypsum underlay, evaporate survey,
in sea of coral tree, beach bums,
and roots so deep they reach
echoes no sea shell can mimic
with fidelity – *inland, inland* –
what is being said, what is being said?
I like aloneness but not loneliness,
and I call those who share
the salt array psychology.

3

Don't forget the granite
decay, the backyard radiation
of the emergent wave,
to wall water to reservoir
where swans tell stories
few hear. I climbed, too,
examined by ornate
rock dragons, and even
a sandalwood decaying
in a sunken island,
gnamma hope.

4 Draining from Lake King

Full-blown infrastructuring of salt.
Harrowing out to channel away
and make the river Camm
thrive again, rock looming
and its lizard eyes taking
in so much salt heaped
to break us down,
preserve us, breathing
with deadwood.

5

Overload of salt – breakout! –
electrolytes of psyche

and weirdness of sleeping
in banks and columns and sinkholes
of salt to bring childhood back,
a thirsty salivating for a lost world
that is not lost was never lost –
that propaganda of 'emptiness',
of 'possession', out of focus.

6

Westerlies rush the failure
of hydrography – waves
on the lake and that warm-
cool differential stirring
memories not mine to have,
and a shuddering of rafters,
funnelling of bricks, and a denial
of isolation even in the lee
a rippling, a lifting of shallows
where sands ply late light
through gnarled trees
and water-branches
bristle a foreboding
armour that lures
with divination
only I can make
false – water is found,
drink in what you can't drink.

7

The inland sea is rising
and the ship of state lists
and capsizes into the eye
          of whirlpool.
Colour-shift rapid
as sun fading on voyages
to where discovery
was presence. Millennia.
A green carpet in dry euphoria.
          Qualities of light
          shifting, slipping
across hot ice on decks.

8 Who to blame?

Morning is the gypsum shift
and visitors play in scalds.

Crunch! on effervescing mirages,
watched from a periphery

of crows, galahs, dusky
wood swallows. *Vut vut*!

Landcare as fences bloom
at bases orange-rose

sheets of grouting, slabs
of render – land's building

coming unstuck, and some
claiming 'lifeless'. *Vut vut*!

I lake, I make lake of me
when I really shouldn't –

compelled as the wind
ruffles lee in memory

of last evening – all sun's
setting ways enraptured

to bleach an easterly rising.
And the old tracked machine

that would have its say,
rusted to return in the broadest

sense (have you ever had to listen
to farm or military machinery

working far into the night?),
partial and immoderate –

once, in its day, it has its say
and it was brine on the blade.

Bloody. *Vut vut*! Bloody.

INTERLUDE

Tim would love it out here.
Tracy would let distress and wonder
mix and rest and intensify.

9 I refuse

I refuse to bend to form
or to a prosody of certainty
when all is vicarious.

Saltbush and pigweed
rustle succulent against
evisceration and the Camm

sighs over its naming
and the slippage as the dry
which lifts its salt to the wind

or grows spikes from deadwood
left to seed. Saltbush replays.
Salt polyphony, bristles.

Sadly, I understand. Sadly
I gorge on the 'qualities
of light'. Crystallography.

10 The revitalising qualities of Salt 'wastes'

A courting couple
new couple
couple on their honeymoon,
a couple kicking up the salt splinters
breaking through to the viscous
soil beneath – it's their moment
in the sun, all modernity's
offerings compacted
into their fun,
the photos they take
of one another,
together.

11

I count syllables of salt,
their slow-fast grieving,
their incitements to love –
the dancing couple
waiting to capture
their kicked-up fuss,
their breaking through to land
that will barely know them,
through the corrosive mask –
briefly vivid, briefly frolicking
in the palaeochannel.

12

Over wave, arched,
on a flared slope
as sheoak enraptured
with run-off still the residue
annexed at the 'joint cleft '
try not to look at the rockwork
as an example of European art
of the twentieth-century –
that new colonial way
in the claims to decolonising –
just know there are other ways,
and claim no more. Where
the rock dragon shifting foot
to foot says, What privacy
am given, on the hunt
for the unsuspecting.

13

Stay clear.

Don't deny.

Crystals

aren't *your*

fortune.

Vut vut!

Vut vut!

Vut vut!

JK

I wish to acknowledge Phil and Len Collard, and the Collard family in general for their generous response to this poem in the context of my writing their country. In doing so, I acknowledge elders past, present and future of the Noongar Boodja I am writing.

The Artlessness of Internal Travel

Going away enforced where I was.
There was no here without there.
The Canning River fed Bull Creek
overshadowed by paperbarks
with its sharp white shore, a cul de sac
fed from the Hills, up over the Scarp.

Or far up the coast, a new home,
the Chapman River ate sandstone
and bream in the pools spoke
upstream language in their stasis.
Away, was religious when religion
was failing me, and I failing it.

Always heading Down South
or Up North, a thread through
a broken marriage, a string cord
between family jam tins, I travelled
to Wheatlands farm and its salt scalds,
to the millionaire's farm near Mullewa
managed by my father and his new wife.
Then to the mining towns of the Pilbara.
Later to a shack in a paddock
on the edge of jarrah forest.

Shells, rocks, cutting of plants,
the odd polaroid, lock-journals
with sketchy notes of departure,
arrival, incidents: Dad hit a roo
not far out of Exmouth after
the cyclone took the roof off
our motel and we sheltered
in the doorframe of the bathroom.

Driving throughout the night,
unloading bricks at Koorda,
then onto Merredin, more bricks …
and then sometime near dawn
the truck off the road, brick packs
broken all over. Swish of gear changes,
hooking the button up alongside the shift,
low, high … a range of habitation
as adversarial as bitumen,
night punctured with headlights.

In the shothole canyon outside Exmouth,
communications remixing my brain chemistry,
its electricity, I got a sense of what it is
to be alone and lost, to drink rock
and dryness, take blue as emptiness.
But to retract and embrace,
and see the fullness of loss.
I am still there, scant vegetation
and presence I can now explain.

Long straights, towards arid zones.
The Pioneer bus with my younger brother,
the flat-tops, the mesas, the emollient of erosion,
the leafiness of banana plantations around Carnarvon
that seemed as artificial as flower arrangements,
the pragmatic wish-fulfilment of tracking stations,
the communities that wouldn't let us in
but we hung around, hoping to travel
where the car wouldn't take us, the Ampol
and Golden Fleece travel paraphernalia
guide us. Quasi-religious. Always quasi.
Wanting to put something back.

And the salt ponds, evaporative vats
granulated tissue of the iron industry,
as hardcore porno sold to teenagers
in supermarkets outwitted blue-ringed octopi,
the tide rushing in over mudcrabs,
swamping mangroves, cobbler lurking
and queenfish out in the channels.
If you behave, we'll drive out
to the anomaly, Millstream.
Water in the gorges contradicts
the dry God you want to worship.
Nothing is 'straggly' because writing
is what I take to it: unwritten
yet, a shimmering affirmation.

Later I would fly on MMA down to Perth.
Filling the map, dragging coast into crops,
a semi-literate overview. Returning with piles
of books, Frank O'Hara made street corners
of topography, silos sucked into his art.

But trips from the farm into a deeper wheatbelt
were memories bereft of the anxieties of connection:
salt scalds widening out beyond fences, speaking
liminal against the grain, hot on the steps
of the translocated, the driven-off.
Further out, defences lowered,
where wodjil tests granite
and rock dragons press sun
into mirrors and the hawk watches,
I announced the crime. In whose footsteps
I follow, and the marks I leave behind: so distinct,
but empty, the yellowing spray-fringe at the edges.

And south, to the tall timber fantasy,
stomping ground of my Irish ancestors,
stomping down karri with vestiges of hunger
and anger, the bitten homeland transference
to lift selkies from king waves, conspire
with the haves and fight off the have-nots
they might become at any moment, travelling
through wetlands where the old farm etched
its way into the buried, tramped down bones.

Bits of language coming through, and straight past
the houses of family I didn't know,
family who knew the wide spaces
between tuarts before the ships arrived.

Or where whales ended up in kettles
and tanks – travelogue of family
friendships – Carnarvon Whaling Station –
grandfather in the spotter, and great white sharks
off Cheynes Beach I intone, carry on about:
but mainly the eternal south, the other blue,
the depth outside ownership, despite all claims.

JK

Edges of Aridity

for the Adnyamathanha people

'Arid' is relative to what grows
in dry places, what thrives in its dirt, its stone,
its air. When water flows here it flows fast,
the rain beads on the surface, fuses
and rushes. A river redgum catches the detritus,
braces the collapsed, the lost, the leftovers.
In its upper branches pink and grey galahs
eye the deep and promising hollows.

When native pines were eaten by the mine's furnaces,
edges shifted. As sheep found the shade of cassia –
the 'wait a while bush' – the edges shifted. A town builds
out of its gatherings, its edges. Moments even out
between the hills, high above sea level, and heat
is the thin edge of a conversation, emu
and kangaroo shape the dry air, the movements
of ants are the movements of mountains, and cicadas
wait for the sun to set, to name the night's arrival.

The edge of town is near its centre, pepper trees
complicate the shade which is always a pleasure – rabbits
on bare slopes of evening kick dust as dry-place smoke.
Out of this, the cemetery is an edge I know – it speaks
to all places of the dead, inside and out. Quartzite, slate

and marble hold the dead down in the copper ground,
but they break through constantly. A whirly whirly –
vigorous, determined – crosses the road, a strong funnel
lifting the scarce pickings of dry ground,
concentrating. It crosses into the cemetery

and connects ground and sky, a spiral nebula
of the dead, a whirlpool of the arid, as the wedge-taileds
catch their thermals, and a rabbit, just out of range
of the spiral, digs at a grave before stopping short
of farmers, miners, and a priest, men, women, and children.
The edges of a space full as sunlight, full of unmarked
and unknown graves, reaching out over the fencelines,
living with the living, part of country. Tin flowers,
headstones bled of script, a fenced spread
or a mine opening, the woodwork splintering
in simulacra or realtime. The edge brought closer

as a garden drinks what's offered. How do we
move on from our dead? And should we? Our days loud
at the grave. Entry and exit, opened and closed. Ironwork,
ironflowers, the polish of stone sheets, segments, steps.
Early morning backgrounds the sounds of white-faced finches,
spiny-cheeked wattle birds, sounds of hill outlines.
No cemetery is silent. They are loud in the heads of locals
and visitors alike. And the dead are loud in their graves.
Edges are beginnings, not ends. I have seen the silhouettes
of backlit ranges, the cracked edges of stars, the living places of the
dead,
the cutlines of flow, the edges of thermals and limestone
and slag heaps, the needles of acacias and their seedpods

opening, hoping new growth will join the old,
and know these edges are beginnings, not ends.
I have heard the tawny frogmouth just out of reach
of the town's lights and seen shadows move out from headstones,
alive, edgy *and* stable, moving out over rock and faultline,
lifting up from below ground flowing rich with aridity.

JK

Reconstruction of the *Foundation of Perth 1829*, Painted by George Pitt Morison for the Centenary of 1929: a poem against ekphrasis

for Kim Scott

And so it begins, the felling,
the transfer of commodities;
a shiny sheoak sewing box
with brass hinges and nine
compartments in royal blue velvet,
a lure to Queen Mary who will bestow
it back on the colonials: such grace,
such cultural largesse.

Mrs Dance and the stone,
Captain Stirling and the tree,
Mrs Dance and the tree,
Captain Stirling and the stone?

So the capital gains. Plenty
of eucalypts and sheoaks
and xanthorrhoeas went down
for the count, as now
with outer suburbs, the axe-blows'
rings doing their decade by decade
expansions. Soldiers for back up.

Levity and redemption,
levering of stone,
grubbing-out of vegetation,
degradations of green

yellowing down to sand,
to burn with summer's hunger
for shade: buildings to replace
the sheltering leaves. Official
speech, pronouncement – enigmatic
endowment, a leap of time
and faith: erasure, insure.

Other women on board
with birthrights (pregnant,
suckling), so Mrs Dance shines
bright: white flare of muslin
as ancestral voices whisper
through smudged leaves
of light, colour, impression,
needled foliage brushed out,
zamias reaching out to botany
underwriting discovery,
attesting herbariums
and all pressed flowers
to traverse in letters,
reading land as what's
familiar in 'river' or
brooding 'sky', figurative
sizing of rank and file:
the eminent, and who sees
a hundred years into the future,
and back further still,
the figures the artist
won't see, won't answer.

As once we sheltered
in the Supreme Court Gardens
between ficus trees and rampant
palms, the law closing in
and skyscrapers funnelling
a vicious sea breeze.
Reach into the basket,
bottles and glasses,
food from the Salvos.

'A swan and wild ducks'
pass by', favours are done
in the retelling: the centennial
picture confirms what they
want, what they've always
known. This is just how
it was. The city gets older
and the paint is restored.
I dreamt I was there: coming
into the picture from nowhere.

Mrs Dance put an axe to me
and the officials all partied
hard long after. Why feel
compelled to apologise
for their behaviour, their joy?

The axeman in shirtsleeves
takes over and finishes
the job with a few well-
aimed strokes. He thinks
of Mrs Dance so near;
I can sense this, being
a heartbeat from both.

Mrs Dance, wife
of the commander
to the ship Sulphur,
'persuaded to venture
so far into savage country'
will surely never
be the same again.

JK

Respect

Mum's friend says that her people
know which of the white families in the district
behaved decently and which didn't,
and memory being what it is means
that long ago or that far back
doesn't erase anything, and the sins
of the past are as much the sins of now
as of the future; when the waterholes and river
went salt the rainbow serpent choked up
and slid off to find the little fresh water left,
hidden in a clump of trees at the base of Mt Matilda,
a place higher up than the salt though still brackish,
collecting from the run-off, pausing between rocks
before seeping down into the dead river; Mum's
friend says that where Mum lives is 'Wendy's place',
which is generous though surely
ironic if taken out of context; and context
is overwhelming though temporarily put to one side
in any conversation in a car travelling to Beverley,
passing Caves Road and looking up at the annealed
path of the serpent, the cauterised antiphony
of farmland, scars through the surveyor's mapping;
as a child I recall passing the camp on the outskirts of town
and asking, and asking I recall getting as close as possible
to the stookers working hay on the farm, fencelines crossing
their lines, as kids my age played away from me,
in the shade – Ballardong people whose language
expanded past English, whose language picked at English
to help the farmers out, who filled in the linguistic geography

below the crop, below the ground where a creek started
and whose song flows up to the dark, transforming
out past the sparks of the fire, the notes of ants sleeping,
cut it down like the brittle stalks.
In Northam the prophecies weltered against the hills
and the protector rounded up people like songs
of praise: Moore River and the absolution
of Christ in the wafer of bread, broken
over roads travelled against the grain;
looking onto Walwalinj – hill that cries – is the slow
whisper of volcanic residue, or hymns sung by local peoples
and those come later, a tribal meeting place
as much as any other, to some; the Nuns were good to us
I heard someone say you said, but either way,
it was a demolition of all values to others
it was an electroshock of myth inversion
and the choicest cuts of land
were dished out for the taking.
Any rights I have over words I cede to you.
The descriptives or instructives
are my damnation too: taking what heat we can
from the electric light, pride in family
achievements: great footballers in the family,
a teacher who speaks across generations and dreamings,
a right to live in the soil we should be buried in.
From space, all the lines are visible: still there,
glowing green and red and ochre, the blue water
as alive as the stories of its awakening,
its place in the hills, its place where kangaroos,
snakes, lizards, and birds drink.
It's clean water. The lines of walking are clear.

JK

Nganayungu Yagu

Nganayungu Yagu
My mother
Belong to me
Always told me
Walk tall and strong
Little Nyarlu me

Nganayungu Yagu
My mother
Belong to me
Always told me
Don't be afraid
In any space
This land is old
Your ancestors' spirits
Will protect you for
They remember all those
Who belong and
Come from it

Nganayungu Yagu
My mother
Belong to me
Now in that land
Her spirit watches
Over me
As I move around
On this our land

CPG

Rain Clouds' Arrival

The arrival of rain clouds
To be welcomed and embraced
For the balance of life
Is wrapped within
Nature's way nothing else
Precious rain to kiss
The face of country
Filling drinking cups of life
Bringing presents to the cycle of growth
And living bush foods flourish
Wildflowers pop up to say hello
Allowing the land to smile
Moving deep over country
To awaken the seeds
To awaken the land
To emerge within rain clouds
Brings more than a sense of renewal,
Refreshing and sustaining
Tracks and memories
Across the land
Across the country
Hold their place

CPG

Lake Joondalup

Suburban disturbance
Rooftops hurting the eye
Messy on the skyline
Evidence of another way
Coloniser's villages
Like sardines in a can
Connected like caterpillars
Crawling closer to the
Lake's water edge
I see birds together
All kinds not moving
Or looking at me the stranger
A feeling in the air
I can't quite describe
Peaceful drawing me in
Then making me
Feel like an intruder
So still so different
To the urban noise
Beyond the trees
Lake Joondalup
Waits for its people

CPG

Old Girl

For Julie Dowling

Old Girl's eyes draw me on first sight
Pulling me close into her presence
I know Old Girl I seen her before
My Aunty, my Nanna, my Cousin
Her eyes have seen much
The sadness and pain
Wrapped tightly within the
Coloniser's cruel practices
Yet Old Girl stands firm
Strong presence despite inside feelings
Pushed deep into a place
Where no one can use
Enough has been done already
To her and her people
And her country in life
Moving forward in life with
Affection respect and loyalty
From those who value her
Old Girl is missed
When those who have a need
For her comfort, security, laughter
Wisdom, guidance or just
For being Old Girl in sight
Her place has not been shifted
Even if her country around her as
Her place has just taken a detour
She was there for them little ones
Even though she may have lost her own

When they cried for mummy and daddy
Old Girl gave them the strength to move
Into the unknown life awaiting
Her smile and mischievousness
Delights the young ones and others
For the harshness of the world
Is softened, tolerable and strengthened
With Old Girl around

CPG

Blue Scar

To push aside the concrete
Bitumen urban mess on country
A cultural mindset continuing
From old people to now
And into the future
For remember a
Whiteman's presence
And laying on country
Does not cancel out or replace
Beliefs, customs or values
These transform in
A physical sense to survive
And re-emerge in some space
In some mark or in some form
To remind you of
The strength and resilience
Of a people belonging

CPG

Simply Yarning

For Dawn Bessarab

Yarning is a beautiful conversation
A time and space allowing
Laughs, tears, happiness, anger
Sadness, seriousness, joking
Or nothing but relaxation
Yarning could be slow
Especially when a cuppa's involved
It could be fast and furious
Like a cascading waterfall
Smashing to the bottom
Hard, rough and dirty
But hey it's worth it
Yarning could be intense and complex
Serene and beautiful
Depends on how you extract
What you want
Or get what you don't want
Yarning is a beautiful conversation
From that moment
That space
That time
Yarning puts us on common ground
Hey come on Dawn let's have a yarn

CPG

Yarn Response Poem

How can I but take up the call,
Charmaine, and yarn right back at you –
it's what we do when we connect,
have a yarn about this and that,
about versions of Gero the white stakeholders
in the town would pile on us like we're
all lucky having any part of it.
And for me, a returnee or a blowback,
my school years still showing
me around the streets, under the thin
shadows of tall Norfolk pines,
ships masts, the offshoots of voyages
of exploration and exploitation.
All that, and family, and art
and stuff. You know, we went
into the Yamaji Art gallery
and bought a couple of paintings
for our son Tim, because they meant
so much to him, the artist also
a teenager, following in her father's footsteps,
and then on to the Julie Dowling
exhibition in the Town Gallery
that you curated. That was powerful
and moving and the costs of work
were like the sea stirred and heard
deep inland. All that, all those stories,
and the women in the Yamaji gallery
saying they knew my brother, Stephen
the muso-artist-surfer-shearer

who loves people, who lives
as much outside capitalism
as anyone I've ever known.
You know him too, and he knows
you, and we all feel good about that.
This is yarning, too, Charmaine,
and I take my cue from you
and celebrate the back & forth,
even a bit of overtalking!

JK

Third Space

Come grab my mara
I dare you come on
What you're not sure
Not sure diversity exists
Not sure diversity is healthy
'We are one … we are Australian'
Crikey turn it off – if you are not sure
Beautiful at school assembly
But everyone will grow up
To see the difference
To see the diversity of cultures
Voices, opinions, attitudes, interpretations
Come on grab my mara
I dare you – come on
See that space over there
It's a third space where we might get on
me space + you space = third space
Oh it's scary alright
Fluid, moving, unsure of what's there
But that's the one space we can
Find common ground
It is somewhere we can
Both own the space
Both share the space
To exist, grow, move forward
To move forward
It's the only space
We can find genuine common ground
Everything else is bullshit

Come on I dare you
Grab my hand
We can discard our
Protective robes of
Biases, superiority, stereotypes
Oh yes don't look surprised
We both own those robes
You wear yours when you
Call me a black multhu, a gin, a black bastard
I wear mine when I call you a
White invading convict land grabbing multhu
Oh yeah we both got those robes
But that space over there
Will allow us to take off the robes
And stitch a new robe
To wear and heal together
On this land we both call home
What you're still not sure
Come on grab my mara
I'll just wait for you over there
For when you are ready

CPG

Ngana Nyinda

Ngana nyinda
Where you from
Who you are
Ngana nyinda
Who your mob
Do they come from far
Ngana nyinda
Who that there
Ngana nyinda
Hey they different mob
From everywhere
Aah different mob
From everywhere
Together
Barndi

CPG

Balayi Mundungu

Balayi Mundungu
Balayi Mundungu
Look out little devils
Everywhere
Sitting on your shoulders
Whispering in your ears
Pinching you hard
When someone different
Strolls by or steps into
Your little yard

Balayi Mundungu
Balayi Mundungu
Poking you in the head
Did you hear what
They made you do
Did you hear what
You just said
About the 'Others'
Different from you
A tear for you
I shed and shed

Balayi Mundungu
Balayi Mundungu
Do be very careful
On common ground

For the little devils
Can bring out your
Prejudices is always around

CPG

On Julie Dowling's *My White Friend*, Geraldton Regional Gallery, 2017

Who do we work for? Who pays up, smiling, friendly-like?
Who has washed and ironed the linen dresses? The altar cloth?

The church is a pyramid and the focus on eternity is a friend's –
we all have friends! – in our shoes or feet vanishing in grasses,
introduced grasses, native grasses, in our halo which might

be good spirit, might be shared might be encompassing
might be a force-field for a truth of two might be an exclusion
zone might be friends' combined energy might be a barrier?
Land walked and walked. Story-places of being always being.

A white friend in a white dress. A white friend that shines
in your glow, reflecting *out* on the viewer studying closely
in the gallery, shifting from foot to shoe, shoe to foot.

Who do we work for? Who pays up, smiling, friendly-like?
Who has washed and ironed the linen dresses? The altar cloth?

JK

The Great Western Woodlands

IM Veronica Brady

I merit merrit and what names
stood longer and will stand again
thin rising to blue sky to charred crow
to red wattlebird and honeyeater
to drown at the foot of waterbush.

Driving east into the Victorian
Mallee, and then the emptiness
of grassed plains that weren't
grassed plains, where trees
are windbreaks to be harvested,
the essence of the Western
woodlands is clarified.
Its loss would be
an act of terror:
those emptying farms
that would come in its stead
blank slabs of old-before-their-time
graves, all creation knocked down.

Quandong is a shrub I was
overly familiar with as a child.
In the woodlands I cherish
it for its fruit, and for itself.
It speaks – listen, listen.
It wants its own space,
gets on well with its neighbours,
can take human projections.

But to be deleted is not in its vision.
It hears the pain of loss
as sandalwood does.

We see a lone emu –
we see a lone roo –
we see a lone eagle –
we see a lone ant
making its way home.
They are going somewhere,
having somewhere to go.
This is more than human
intuition. This with the certainty
of a Dundas mahogany
rising out of quartz,
feeling the workings
of the hole-in-the-ground
nearby. Nibbling away.

This great lung,
this great mind,
this great flesh and blood
and cellulose entity
is the powerhouse –
it is the vastly regional,
it is the specific and inclusive,
it is the everything we are.

JK

Blue Hazmat Suits in the Coolbellup Bush Prior to its Destruction

A premonition or a delayed reaction?
A parody of deaths from blue asbestos,
fibres invading Tracy's father's lungs,
and lungs of so many others we've known.

And as the wound is widened, stretched
by sadists, blue hazmat suits are seen
bobbing in and out of the undergrowth,
a consummate piece of pastoral diplomacy

played out on crown land, a colonial
power trip for the born-again remittance men,
their shock troops without masks
breathing deep the dust from the dozer,

from the mulcher; O lèse-majesté flexes
as the arrests mount and fibres fall out
and about, confetti for this wedding
of development and annihilation,

such comfortable bedfellows. And
so the evidence mounts, the bushland
is riddled with dumped asbestos products,
the tests verify, and then evidence

is suppressed, misplaced, dispersed,
deleted. O fibres dispersed throughout
the suburbs into lungs of all ages, all conditions,
do you expect us to be grateful?

And still the juggernaut, transparency
of fences revealing the antiworld,
where ghosts prevaricate, disorientated.
Children breathe here, you bastards.

And remember that smug capitalist
eating asbestos on his breakfast cereal?
Publicity stunt, but some bought it.
Softly softly among the rowdy machines.

Fibres beneath fingers.
Fibres in noses, mouths, lungs.
Fibres on clothes, on uniforms taken home,
dispersed among loved ones.

JK

Cathedral Avenue

This doesn't have to be a requiem,
no, not yet. Each breath these strong
old trees let us have is a breath that keeps
us going, keeps the pieces of belonging in place.

What is held in the cathedral
of salmon gums and wandoo?
The branches reach to hold
the sky in place, to keep

earth and sky connected.
Prayers in all languages
and all faiths collect in their
illustrative branches, echo in hollows –

all creatures that come and go,
that make life in their outreach
help us hear and see who we are,
singing past present future.

And the owl knows the cockatoo
and a galah cocks its comb at the sun;
the shade translates the writing of time
which the machinery would cut short.

JK

Sammies (Salmon Gums)

for Lindsay, Tim, Tracy and Kim

And so the ancient salmon gums are killed off – death-wish
where roads are widened to 'prevent deaths'?

East of where I write but not too far east
the great sammies arch over the road
to hold movement in, work to keep a grip
on the land as they knew it two hundred
or three hundred years ago, ringing
the changes of timeline owned and owning,
knowing patterns of seasons from voices
rising beneath them always, and so wide
in the trunk that two of us can only just
touch hands, a difficulty the plastic ribbons
of the clearers, sashed around, don't have –
not 'welcome back' from war but declarations
of war. Strips of dried bark crunching
          reminders underfoot.

If you've never seen a sammie in its home
place, never been haunted and rejuvenated
by the way it works dawn or evening light,
then you probably can't know how much
its deletion diminishes you, never mind
country itself. You'll have equivalents,
of course, but there's no analogy
to be drawn that won't dilute the agency of light,
of that orange-pink-white-brown bark negotiating

temporal and spatial variables. Hands reaching
to touch, a nest high above makes glyphs.
Sammies, poured into their columns,
ribbed vaults, horizons of canopy
through which land and sky parley.

You know, near those magnificent sammies …
You know, those sammies umbrella-ing
near the corner with Station Road, *you know*,
you know. In the hot wind scouring
bleached paddocks, embrace
their cool forms. A heart stretched
out, an anatomy of transfiguration.
We acknowledge the elders, who know
the name of all the creatures who dwell
in their inner and outer worlds, cross over.
We acknowledge the poverty we make
in taking them away, these sammies.
Where the cropping went, the sammies fell.
        Their characters inflections of soil.

Riding beneath, rewritten by the spirals of shadow.
Leaning against the base of a thick trunk to shelter
from a sun that would hallucinate you to walk
straight into flames. Slowly, cautiously, drinking
from the waterbag, you scry a future bare of the present.
Picnics, gatherings, knowledges of healing and origins,
all learning cut to the base, grubbed out. Always
these paradoxes like cigarettes ashed out of car
windows at the height of summer, flickers
of holocaust in such a casual gesture. Sammies
        see us looking out for ourselves.

East of where I write but not too far east
the great sammies arch over the road
to hold movement in, and in our mind's eye
we wander though the ambulatory, cars
rushing past. We are three generations
of onlookers enraptured by ancient trees
that make settlement look as tenuous
as it is. Knowing this, we listen to the pink
& greys, the Port Lincoln parrots, the honeyeaters,
the black-faced wood swallows, the willy wagtails,
the array of insect species, the Wurak, the Wurak, the Wurak,
which we borrow from a language that keeps these
trees in the constellations and *won't* let go of the roots deeper
than light, as far as we understand it, wanting
        to learn, to respect.

JK

Still Shame – Why?

Too shame to dance
Nyambi so pretty
Too shame to sing
Mamagarrimanha lifts the spirit
Too shame to talk
Wangga so beautiful
Too shame to write
Bibarlu wangga powerful
Too shame to mix
Yamaji lovely people
Too shame still why
This world needs to
See all beautiful Yamaji
And Yamaji need to
See the world

CPG

Strong Wajarri Man

His skin is fair – no argument there
Lived as a Yamaji all his life
As a strong Wajarri man
That is his world that is his clan
Though he was raised in town
This family know their connections
To kin, place, country all around

His skin is fair – no argument there
His old people's sweat and tears
Dropped into Wajarri land
His old people's feet
Stirred Wajarri sand and dust
Their bones now rest
On Murchison stations out there
And some now say no to this Wajarri man
For Wajarri land he can't care
Cause he not related to them
That type of reason is up in the air

His skin is fair – no argument
He is heading to 70 a winja now
He knows his barna and clan
For he is a strong Wajarri man

CPG

Identity Police

A word of warning
Mr Mrs Identity Police
Watch the words
You might regret
Be very careful
What you say
To the fair skinned Yamaji
Don't cruel them or
Dismiss them like that
One day this could be how your
Grand kids, great grandkids
Are treated because of a colour thing
Taunted, dismissed, dissected, cruelled
Think about that next time
Learn to ssshhh … shut your mouth
Don't let them words you might regret
Escape into the wind
Push them back … hold them
Yeah be very careful what you say
Anyways who are you to say
Who is real and who is not
Who can be and who cannot
Learn to ssshhh … shut your mouth
It's not your right to be the identity police
There are words you might regret

CPG

Drug Slaves

The most hated people
In our communities
Should be the drug dealers
And drug couriers
The ones who risk
The highways carting drugs
The ones who give the first shot
The ones who give the first taste
To our beautiful healthy strong young ones
To our future leaders we carry forward
The ones soak up a hellish status
Display of cars and motorbikes
Rings and gold chains around their necks
Not too flashy but flashy enough
The ones who are not strangers
To a community but rather
Our brothers, sisters, cousins, uncles, aunties
Grandmothers, grandfathers, friends, children
Thinking only of the dollar they can get
Or drug access for their own habits
When will they get shown
The other side of their sales
The broken minds
The broken bodies
The broken souls
The broken homes
The broken communities
They should be the most hated

CPG

Needle Teacher

Oh I have heard the whispers
About what a great teacher she is
That she is gentle
Knows how to handle a needle
Smooth as it finds a vein
Does it herself no problem
A drug dealer's prize
She will take away your fears
Of injecting yourself
She will teach you
Once you get the taste
So that you can introduce
Others to a hellish space
Oh I have heard the whispers
Better than a nurse they say
(No one is better than a nurse who saves lives)
The needle teacher fucking everyone up
The wicked witch of the speed world

CPG

Dark Light Bulbs

Pardon my ignorance
I always though light bulbs
Were to lighten up a space
Make things brighter
Help us to see better
Now I find they have
A sinister dark side

They are a tool to hell
Don't try and tell me otherwise
A speed freak's, rev head's
Smoking instrument
To extinguish the goodness
From head and body
Whose dark idea was this?
To allow pain and misery
From something that creates brightness

Light bulbs have many purposes
But this one I have seen
Is evil and fucked
I know this cos of family
I seen my young relatives
Going crazy losing it
Young men and young women
Unnaturally thin
Mood swings like you would
Never believe
Teeth rotting, track marks

Pardon my ignorance
I always though light bulbs
Make things brighter
Whose dark idea was that?

CPG

Death Stress

The gut wrenching feeling of death
Tugs you to the very core
There is too much in the community
The flow is way too fast
If you don't scream aloud
You scream deep within
Where only you can feel
Your body shaking
Your spirit like a restless
Thing trapped in a cage
Tormented feeling death
So close and so often

Their reasons for departing
Heart attack, diabetes, stroke
Does not matter in the end
What matter is that
They will no longer tread
Upon the soft earth with you
That they will no longer
Hug you when you need it
Is what matters
That they will no longer
Tease and joke with you
Is what matters
Their reasons for departing
Do not matter in the end

Forced tears is what we have
We have cried too much
Forced tears is what is here
With our family dying way too fast
Most times way too young
Sometimes not making sense
We suffer death stress
Not enough time to grieve
For each of those who leave
Not enough time to heal
Forced tears to show it's real
Forced tears is sometimes
All that is left as we struggle
We suffer death stress
We grieve for ourselves as well

CPG

Funeral Directors

Many know the process well
How to organise a funeral
Is not a stranger after a while
The real funeral directors are kind
Patient, sympathetic, respectful
It's their job isn't it?
And it can be a costly one at that
Some wanting more than they can afford
Coffins can be expensive
Yagu wanted a simple dignified funeral
And a coffin in the colours
It was found in Noongar country
Making anxious funeral directors
They hadn't done this before in Geraldton
Yagu wanted to decolonise funeral ceremony
And this was her way of doing it
Many of us know the process well
It is a stressful but respectful one
Becoming unofficial funeral planners
Every family has a funeral planner
We have become friends with burials
To help our loved ones, our friends, our community

CPG

Monitoring Lizards

Five hundred will do it mate
To walk this land
Monitoring lizard over
Rocks, hills and sand
Clearing the way for
Train tracks, pipelines, roads
Mine sites, power lines, land release
Clearing land – no sites here mate
Five hundred dollars will do it mate
Heritage site clearances
A trap for the poor
Lollies for the lizards
You know them ones who
Sell their country for the dollar
Five hundred bucks in the pocket
Will bring some food, grog and gunja
Or casino, casino, casino, casino
Jobs for the boys, jobs for the men
Monitoring for the robbers
And their false plans

CPG

A New Ode to Westralia: Anthem for All Future Sporting Events

The state is killing our souls
The state has murdered the people – some they murder over and over
The state has deployed vicious antibodies to kill the good cells
and let the infection thrive
The state has equated work with destruction and manipulated the outcome –
remember, the state has no love for unions.
The state deployed its shock troops who watched on as poems were yelled
at them, their commander marshalling attitude, saying: how can we
shut this one up? Poets of the world, take notice. They will close
you down the moment you break free of your anthologies,
your safety in pages of literary journals, the comforts
of award nights.
The state shapes itself out of dust rising from underforest's
soul exposed to the exhaust of earth-moving equipages
The state chips and mulches because it has heard rumours of Plato's
theory of forms and thinks it needs a new translation full of local
business inflection, full of their own brand of civilisation.
The state has no intention of letting traditional owners maintain traditional
places of worship of culture or belonging – it's always been about
the twin poles of denial and deletion.

The state has reservoirs of species names and the odd pressed sample
of a flower they wish to remain as a Latin name and a collectible,
gathering in worth, which is the essence of market economics,
rolling on through the bushland with gung-ho in-your-face finality.
The state wants you to gasp as the tall tree cracks and is brought down fast,
the pair of tawny frogmouths lifting to nowhere, dazzled by daylight.

JK

Always thieves

Thieves arrived in all disguises
Colonial officers, convicts, settlers, free men
No treaties and trinkets here
Guns and guns was their dirty talk
Thieves wrapped warmly with the
Blankets of terra nullius

Arrived as colonial thieves
                    Remain as colonial thieves

Stealing, tricking, lying, murdering
Claiming all lands for the king
A crown dripping with Aboriginal blood
A bloodied history worthy of thieves
Passed on generation after generation

Arrived as colonial thieves
                    Remain as colonial thieves

Handing out land grants to settlers
Auctioning land to all except the invisible victims
Was this not an empty land free for the taking?
Massacres were strategic for any interference
This my friend is how White Australia did it
This my friend is Australia's history

Arrived as colonial thieves
                    Remain as colonial thieves

Thieves remain in all disguises
Mining companies, politicians, governments
With their greedy white, yellow, white hands
Dirty hands coated with traces of blood
From the past from the present from the land
Selling to the highest bidder

Arrived as colonial thieves
                    Remain as colonial thieves

CPG

In Marapikurrinya: for Ms Dhu

The uniforms won't listen, ore heaped up,
long steel ships waiting to take country
away. They refuse to see themselves,
boots and all, march away

from all spirits. They laugh at body,
they laugh at words, but they
have no idea they are dead-in-themselves,
their faces dressed up for the cameras.

They kill with impunity. They are designed
that way. In another lock-up, I have
seen the body of a young Noongar bloke
tossed like a hessian sack, his bones

all busted, and the ring-a-ring-a-rosie
circle laughing and saying you deserve
what you get. The uniforms denied he was
in there, inside his own body. The sounds

that crept out were television – they all watched
American cop shows. It's all there for them –
the land dressed up as state or nation:
they fancy their long arms reaching out,

they fancy their long arms reaching
across tribal boundaries, heaping it all
into the belly of those long ships
or into trucks or train. To furnaces.

Stretching fences across stone and sand
and far into sea? Their magnificent
jurisdiction. They are their own
totems. They worship their order.

I know that port. I have been in a house
where Nyangumarta and Yamaji
came together listening to Coloured Stone
and Sonny Terry and Brownie McGhee.

And stories were told then, back
then, as the death-toll rises and those
hunting parties of the Old North
find their latest manifestation.

This reaches out to you, Ms Dhu,
and to all those from past and present
who hold you close, who won't
see you lost in the files.

You will outlive them all.
You will hold back the uniforms
from striking more and more of your people down.
You will be the beginning. You will never end.

JK

Growing

For I have been a caterpillar
Far too long cocooned
I lay still in the same space
Waited patiently for the wings
That I knew would grow
And become a part of me
I never wanted to be a caterpillar
But it is part of the journey
Some caterpillars never
Get their wings and it
Is them I fear the most
For they will surely kill us

CPG

Shopping Centre Carpark

So I'm pulled up under the shade of a sugar gum
in the Woollies carpark in Northam, and this guy
pulls up in a car next to me, getting what shade
he can. Our windows are down and I call across
and say, Gidday mate, just wondering if I can ask
your opinion about something. Sure mate, he calls
back, his arms still resting on the steering wheel.
Well, I say, This guy was just asking me – came
up out of nowhere to ask – how much pressure
a ride-on lawn-mower tyre can take. Look, he's
over there now at the servo and is about to inflate
the tyre and I said I reckon 8 pounds and I don't
want to have given him the wrong info. Yeah,
mate, he said, That'd be about right. And then
we joke about the consequences of over-inflation
but at no one's expense. And then we get talking
about double-gees puncturing bike tyres and tricks
to beat the spikes, and how bad they are this year
with the summer rains and he tells me he was
up in Kal doing his work and his dog couldn't
leave the verandah because of them. When I was
wandering the paddocks as a kid, I say, It was
hell – feet like pincushions. And he says, I'm
always tellin' my kids that if you don't check
your shoes we'll have them further than everywhere.
It's a good conversation. Then his family
appear and I return to listening to the radio
before looking up on hearing laughter and seeing
a shopping trolley escaping across the carpark.

My new friend, his family secure in the car,
drives towards the trolley – the carpark is basically
empty, it being a Sunday arvo, just someone approaching
on foot but a dozen car-lengths away – and deftly
grabs the trolley's handle out of his window
and guides it with the car to a line of other trolleys,
slotting it perfectly in place like a nest of tables, a set
of Russian dolls, a magic box. He then drives off
and I think, Well done mate. I wish you a double-gee-
free day. But then a stranger is at my window,
and straight in my ear, There goes trouble,
she spits. Sorry? I say. You know, *that lot …*
I click. I reckon he did an excellent job, I say
back, staring past her into a distance she
won't register. She persists, *They're* trouble.
You've got that wrong, I say, A good bloke
who did a good job. She walks away, saying,
Well I s'pose it's better than leaving the trolley
in the middle of the carpark. And I think over
this town with its abundance of Pauline Hanson's
One Nation signs, and I think over this town and its
foul history, and I think over this town and the friend
I have made, and I say to myself, Brother, if you ever
read this, know I admire you, know I appreciate
your talking over that issue. You know
about the politics of double-gees,
and I am listening to all that you tell me.

JK

*

Shopping Centre Carpark (Response)

For Debbie and Glenda

Geraldton Woollies carpark fringe
Big mob hang out there often
A bottle shop across the road and taxi rank
Good central spot to catch up if you want
Pauline Hanson came to town and went
Across to the carpark fringe shaking hands
Photo opportunity with Yamaji people
For the WA state election train wreck
They didn't know the community
Any group of Aboriginals will do attitude
Three Yamaji women parked up in carpark
And went to do an unwelcome to country
Yes you heard right – an unwelcome to country
For Pauline Hanson One Nation Party
Centre bosses pushed them out
But they refused to retreat to Woollies carpark
With their *get off Yamajiland Pauline H* banner
That party is one big Australian double-gee
As a kid I would call them jubaal-gees
I was a bit shocked to learn proper name
Out bush you gotta have thick skin
Drag your barefoot to minimise hurt
Did that as a kid but now my feet are soft
A bit too soft from wearing shoes nowadays

CPG

The Wild Colonial Boy

The wild colonial boy is a loner
The wild colonial boy has guilt over his plunder
The wild colonial boy plunders his guilt
The wild colonial boy doesn't know
    what to do with the plunder
The wild colonial boy offloads the plunder
    at the trash and treasure
The wild colonial boy can't tune into the Eureka Stockade
The wild colonial boy tries to fly in and fly out but is caught out,
    amphetamines in his urine
The wild colonial boy shares a cell with a Noongar bloke
    who shares law and knowledge from country
The wild colonial boy would rather be inside than out
    because the chains and slavery of the languages
    of occupation leave him confused and angry,
    but inside is murder and he knows it
The wild colonial boy doesn't know what to do
    with his skill set – he thinks of going bush
The wild colonial boy watches the numbats
    near the huts in the visitors' part of Dryandra Forest
The wild colonial boy listens to the crested pigeon flying, to the
  bush stone-
    curlew stalking, the western gerygone singing along with the
    elegant parrot in the canopy and the golden whistler
    and even the nest-hunting shining bronze-cuckoo
The wild colonial boy couldn't be said to be distracted as the cops
    close in around him, but listening to the cross-talk
    of community, the close-knit interferences of belonging,
    the distress of songs broken up by songs of repair and
      reparation

The wild colonial boy is taken and cuffed and has the shit
  kicked out of him – now he is tattooed with a constellation
  that shines over no part of the earth but is permanent
The wild colonial boy watches a young Noongar bloke being beaten
  to death in the lockup
The wild colonial boy has been extradited as witness
  to be laughed at by the judge, to be warned to say nothing
    more
  if he ever wants to wander the plains again
The wild colonial boy promises himself he will shout the truth
  at every footy match, in front of every television,
  to the writers of reports who will go home to love and calm
The wild colonial boy wanders the port streets on his release,
  not understanding he's in a decolonising world,
  the shops bristling with worldly goods, with opportunities,
  and all good things coming to those standing and waiting
The wild colonial boy stops in front of a travel agency window
  and sees a jet will take him anywhere in the world
  and that he can unlearn the codes of his failings –
  he can become he can become he can become
The wild colonial boy has worn dresses and wandered naked
  and has never been stuck on the codes of the pub
  and wonders if his time has come, but the urbane laugh
  at him – his phonelessness – head-in-hands on the kerb
The wild colonial boy looks out for his mate the actor
  but knows in his heart that his friend is gone,
  a friend who had been eaten by *Australia*,
  a friend whose name he won't use in a song
  out of respect for the dead
The wild colonial boy looks out from near the walls
  of the Roundhouse and finds solace
  in the sea, the dolphins, the gulls

The wild colonial boy hears the many conversations
and all languages make sense to him
though he claims none – he is homeless
and stateless and his family can't reach him
The wild colonial boy can't call Australia home, though he has never
really left its shores; but he has travelled outside its jurisdictions,
and he has travelled far beyond its metaphors

JK

A White Colonial Boy

The wild white colonial boy
Arrived with the settlers
Sits at the table of invasion
Drinking regrets and dreams
In a colony of wild visions
This was and is his lot

The wild white colonial boy's
Multiple personalities
Drive him like a madman
Across the generations
I met him personally
A few times over the years
Whispering in my ears
'Why do your people stink?'
Touching the colours on my wrist
Publicly telling me
'My grandfathers raped your grandmothers'
He got a black eye that night from my shoe
A gift from my many grandmothers

The wild white colonial boy
Like a bigshot cowboy in a one-horse town
With steel caps stamping mob to the ground
Digging deep into their back with brutal force
In a cell where inmates become invisible
Becoming a surname, cell name, number
And a caged animal to be played with
By their deranged colonial delights

The wild white colonial boy
Gets wrapped in a sense of
Social media security with the likes
Comments validating his crimes
Committed or about to be
'Thumb ups mate – go ahead it's fine'
Murdering and harming First Nations
In the most horrific and horrendous ways
A murder will become a traffic offence
An unpaid fine will become a murder
And like an audience at a caged arena fight
The social media clowns applaud
A biased court system
Already in favour of the wild colonial boy

The wild white colonial boy perches
Like false king on his high court judge bench
Inflicting further colonial trauma on
Behalf of the Australian government
If First Nations cannot prove continued
Connection to country since invasion
They remain invisible and the justifications
For stealing First Nations' land is safe
The rallies for human justice are
Likened to a community noise for
Which these false kings will not bow down
The concept of terra nullius remains
Intact in the midst and mind of this civilised
Wild white colonial boys' club
And will continue to guide the rules
Of a society and a nation
The wild white colonial boys

Become the very rich of this country
Living the life of colony chaps
Reading outdated books at colonial posts
The colony past has not left anything good
On First Nation relationships
These boys interfere in the welfare
Of First Nations' community and society
Whilst continuing to steal land resources
Wanting to impose bandaid social
Engineering solutions creating further hindrance

As a Mullewa school kid I once sang
A song about a wild colonial boy
Who had robbed the wealthy and helped the poor
An Irish boy shot dead at 21 years young
That's the real wild colonial boy

CPG

Peacocking at Ellendale Pool

Speaking a truth doesn't disabuse
as the martins and swallows fly in & out

of the cliffs, and the pool that is bottomless
reaches beyond all prospects of drought,

and the kestrel positions itself for the edges
of chaos, and campers wade into amoebic

meningitis – into the cells – on a thirty-eight
degree day. Randolph Stow is celebrated

on a sign in the eye of the land, and we are informed
that he wrote *A Haunted Land* and *desire*

troubled this enclave, eye of the fillet,
its bloodied history. And then he was gone,

ensconced in Suffolk, away from his troubled
identity, or the lapses in identity that left

him stranded. And among those revenant
thick white river redgums (felled so readily), caravans

& willie wagtails, and a long-nosed dragon
in a swamp sheoak flashing point to point,

and the public gorging itself on the scene,
that interlude in a thermonuclear world,

pastoral country up to its edges, and another sign
speaking of the 'Indigenous connection' – thriller

subtext, crime drama, blockbuster and award winner,
as if it's a connection we might take under advice!

This land that never stopped being Aboriginal land,
and *it* allows us to walk its erosions without being

plunged to the bottom of the bottomless pit.
Such decorations of the literary! Such gifts of English!

JK

Creation Markings – Ellendale Pool

Mesmerising natural waterhole
Attention commanding rock face
Ancient resident reflects self on water
Open eyes see land talking back

Skimming water surface dragonflies
David Uniapon makes me think

Amangu cultural site drowned
Stubbie to quench thirst on ledge
Water playground farming work ground
Tourist furniture barbie toilet swings

Bimara resting place of creator
Significant culture marker demoted tourism

Bottomless pit conversations
Known to swallow men down darkness
Greenough Tourist Drive cultural marker
With offers of a hidden oasis for intruders

Pick up sand and throw in belonging marking
Protection marking cultural beliefs intact

Tapestry of coexistence woven
Colonised story forefront story
Mythical track moving across land dissected
Metal sculpture appeases society guilt

CPG

Epilogue

As the Beeliar bushland is mowed down
and some of us who aren't traditional owners
are also torn from the inside out, we look to those
whose Boodja it is to take it back, to give it health.
There can be no surrender of spiritual rights
in an agreement made by a government
using bargaining chips they stole
in the first place. Noongar land
yarning with all living things of the world
joined together: land, water, air, spirit.

*

Refuse to hit your head for sadness
Refuse to draw head blood for grief
Refuse to consider death of our land
This barna – our ancestors' land – our land
Exists as long as we exist to protect it
Farmers poison with fertilisers
Salt pans across the wheat belt country
Like seeping green, pink and white wounds
Miners blow up and steal country from country
Property developers bulldoze for urban sprawl
Most Bluff Point shell middens long gone
Consumerism demands highways
Engineers are agents of change – wetlands die
Shall I hit my head to draw blood
To drip into the barna and mix
Letting country know we care

That a sadness exists for settlers don't care
Our ancestors earth memories
Mingled within the grains of country
Are being removed and destroyed
Our old people's spirits are embedded
In a way colonisers can't understand
So I shall hum a lullaby and share a story
To soothe the hurt and pain down generations
A gentle whisper from the past
Visits me in my dreams
Or is it the future that I see
Why are we still invisible?

JK & CPG

CPG: Glossary

Amangu traditional name of cultural group in City of Greater Geraldton area
Balayi is the Wajarri word for a warning, lookout, beware
Balu is the Wajarri word for him, her or it
Barna is the Wajarri word for ground, earth, sand, country
Barndi is the Wajarri word for good, okay, well, clever
Bibarlu is the Wajarri word for paper
Mamagarrimanha in Wajarri means dancing, corroboree
Mara is the Wajarri word for hand
Mooniemia is the traditional placename of Northampton, Western Australia
Multhu is the Wajarri word for vagina
Mundungu is the Wajarri word for devil, creature, ghost
Naaguja traditional name of cultural group in City of Greater Geraldton, Chapman Valley area
Nganayungu in Wajarri means 'my, mine, for, me'
Ngatha is the Wajarri word for I
Nhanda traditional name of cultural group Northampton area
Nhanagardi traditional name of cultural group in City of Greater Geraldton area and in Wajarri means 'over there'
Nyambi is the Wajarri word for dance, traditional type dance shaking knee
Nyarlu is the Wajarri word for woman, female, and girl
Nyinda is the Wajarri word for you (singular), 2nd person
Tangi is the Maori word which refers to a ceremonial Maori funeral or wake
Wadjemup is the traditional placename for Rottnest Island Western Australia
Wangga is the Wajarri word for talk

Winja is the Wajarri word for old, senior
Yagu is the Wajarri word for mother, mother's sister
Yamaji is Wajarri word to describe person of the Midwest/ Murchison region of Western Australia, or Wajarri name for 'man', 'Aboriginal'

JK: Notes

Joseph Bradshaw was a pastoralist who came across numerous rock paintings in the Kimberley in 1891. It is offensive they bear his name. These Gwion Gwion rock art works of the Kimberley are focussed around the Roe River and are said to be up to 25,000 years old. Unique and complex, they evade 'European' analysis in so many ways. For more information readers might see (among other sites): https://www.creativespirits.info/aboriginalculture/arts/bradshaw-gwion-gwion-rock-art

Serment du Jeu de paume – 'The Tennis Court Oath', 20th June 1789, France (in the context of the French Revolution)
See: https://en.wikipedia.org/wiki/Tennis_Court_Oath
Wuruk (or Wurak) is the Noongar word for Salmon gum (*Eucalyptus salmonophloia*)
Boodja is the Noongar word for country
See: https://www.noongarculture.org.au/language/
Bungarra is a sand monitor, sometimes called a 'racehorse goanna'
'Mons. Hawes had a great affinity with the Aboriginal people of Mullewa but they were not comfortable in attending Mass in the local church.' http://www.monsignorhawes.com.au/thebuildings_mullewaoutlady.html

Acknowledgements

CPG

Southerly, Best Australian Poems 2016, Angelaki, Cordite Poetry Review, Australian Book Review, Fremantle Press, Anton Blank Ltd, City of Joondalup.

The poem 'Rain Clouds' Arrival' was written in response to the following artwork by artist Shane Pickett: *The Arrival of Mugaroo's Rain Clouds* 2003, acrylic on canvas, courtesy of the City of Joondalup Collection, as part of Joondalup NAIDOC 2015.

The poem 'Old Girl' was as written in response to the following by artist Julie Dowling: *Old Girl* 2003, courtesy of the City of Joondalup Collection, as part of Joondalup NAIDOC 2015.

The poem 'Blue Scar' was as written in response to the following by artist Ben Pushman: *Blue Scar* 2003, courtesy of the City of Joondalup Collection, as part of Joondalup NAIDOC 2015.

Charmaine wishes to thank and acknowledge her sons Mark and Tamati, all her family, colleagues and friends for their continued support, her First Nation Australian Writers' Network family, her Edith Cowan University alumni peers, her Yamaji Art peers, and John for the decade of conversations. Charmaine thanks Rachel Bin Salleh and Marcella Polain for their commitment, copyediting and assistance, and a special thanks to Magabala Books. She also wishes to acknowledge the Yamaji barna and culture which holds her, especially the barna of the Southern Yamaji on which she writes.

JK

Southerly, Best Australian Poems 2016, Angelaki, Griffith Review, Mutually Said (Blog), *Bush Slam* (Australian Broadcasting Corporation Television), *The West Australian* newspaper.

JK wishes to thank Charmaine, his partner Tracy Ryan, his son Tim, his mother Wendy, and the Ballardong Noongar people whose land he lives on and the Yamaji people on whose land he once lived on. He thanks Rachel Bin Salleh and Marcella Polain for their commitment, copyediting and patience with his particular way of doing things. He also wishes to acknowledge, Ms Dhu's family and all peoples whose land he has written, and to whom he is indebted in all things. And special thanks Magabala Books.